Antonio Vivaldi
The Four Seasons

With the original sonnets and a recording by the
Philharmonia Virtuosi
Richard Kapp, Conductor ◆ Paul Peabody, Violin

THE METROPOLITAN MUSEUM OF ART

Bulfinch Press/Little, Brown and Company
Boston ◆ New York ◆ London

Published by The Metropolitan Museum of Art and Bulfinch Press
Bulfinch Press is an imprint and trademark of Little, Brown and Company (Inc.)

ISBN 0-87099-895-1 (MMA)
ISBN 0-8212-2617-7 (Bulfinch)

Library of Congress Catalog Card Number 99-72282

Concept by Richard Kapp
Translation of the sonnets from the Italian by Douglas and Maura Biow

Produced by the Department of Special Publications,
The Metropolitan Museum of Art: Robie Rogge, Publishing
Manager; Judith Cressy, Project Editor; Anna Raff, Designer;
Lauren Wolfe, Editorial Assistant; Rosemary Hanson, Production.
All photography by The Metropolitan Museum of Art Photograph
Studio unless otherwise noted.

PRINTED IN JAPAN
First Edition
06 05 04 03 02 01 00 99   5 4 3 2 1

Cover: FANTASTIC LANDSCAPE (detail)
Francesco Guardi, Italian, Venetian, 1712–1793
Oil on canvas; 61¼ x 74½ in.
Gift of Julia A. Berwind, 1953   53.225.4

Title page: FÊTE CHAMPÊTRE
Louis Nicholas van Blarenberghe, French, 1716–1794,
and Henri Joseph van Blarenberghe, French, 1741–1826
Painting on vellum; 2⅛ x 3 in.
Gift of J. Pierpont Morgan, 1917   17.190.1152

Right: THE DISPATCH OF THE MESSENGER
François Boucher, French, 1703–1770
Oil on canvas; oval, 12⅝ x 10½ in.
Gift of Mrs. Joseph Heine, in memory of her husband, I. D. Levy, 1944   44.141

Following the Seasons
In Music and Sonnets

When Antonio Vivaldi (1678–1741) was a youth in Venice, the city was one of the great music capitals of the world. Vivaldi learned to play the violin as a boy, perhaps from his father, who was both violinist and barber. A position as music master at the Ospedale della Pietà—an orphanage and school for girls—first brought Vivaldi to public attention. But from about 1705 onward, he was known for his instrumental and operatic compositions, which he performed in courts, salons, and opera houses throughout Europe. Few of his compositions, however, came close to achieving the status of *The Four Seasons*.

The Seasons are the first four concertos of Vivaldi's opus 8, *The Contest of Harmony and Invention*. Written in the early 1720s, the concertos gained a widespread following after 1725, when the score was published by Michel Charles Le Cène of Amsterdam, one of the most prestigious music publishers in Europe. A best-seller in Amsterdam, *The Four Seasons* was also licensed for reprinting in Paris.

The printed version of the concertos included something that the original manuscript had not: four thematic sonnets. In dedicating the score to one of his patrons, Count Wenzel von Morzin of Bohemia, Vivaldi wrote, ". . . I have thought [the concertos] worthy of publication because, in fact, they are more substantial because they are accompanied by their sonnets, which contain an absolutely clear declaration of all the things that are depicted in these works." No one knows who wrote the sonnets. They appeared in full on the opening pages of the edition, each line preceded by a key letter: A, B, C. Someone reading the score could look for the corresponding letter above the appropriate phase of music, and identify all the images that Vivaldi had in mind.

In this special edition of *The Four Seasons*, presented as a book and compact disc recording by the Philharmonia Virtuosi, the sonnets appear both in the original Italian and in translation. They have been paired with masterpieces of Rococo art from the collections of The Metropolitan Museum of Art. All of the works are drawn from the places that *The Four Seasons* was first enjoyed—Italy, France, the Netherlands—and all celebrate the seasons as they were experienced in Vivaldi's own time.

VIOLIN, LONG PATTERN
Antonio Stradivari,
Italian, Cremona,
1644–1737
Spruce, curly maple,
ebony, pearwood;
$23^{1}/_{4}$ x $7^{3}/_{4}$ in., 1693
Gift of George Gould,
1955   55.86

Art in Vivaldi's Venice

The years of Vivaldi's widespread acclaim coincided with a brilliant flourishing in the visual arts in Venice, unparalleled since the golden age of Giorgione, Titian, and Veronese, some two hundred years earlier. The Venetian artistic circle was crowded with luminaries. Sebastiano Ricci and Giambattista Piazzetta, painters of monumental mythological and religious canvases; the view painters Canaletto and Francesco Guardi; the genre painter Pietro Longhi; and the portraitist Rosalba Carriera all hailed from Venice. The city was also home to the most celebrated artistic genius of the eighteenth century, Giambattista Tiepolo, heir to the sparkling pictorial pagentry of Veronese.

Of the various genres of painting produced in Venice in the eighteenth century, none is more paradigmatic than the *veduta*—the depiction of views of the Venetian lagoon and mainland. First practiced in Venice by Luca Carlevaris, the *veduta* became the specialty of Canaletto and his contemporary Francesco Guardi. Both artists produced scores of paintings and drawings—and, in Canaletto's case, etchings—that showed dazzling panoramas. The urban and rural scenery also spawned a fanciful type of landscape known as the *capriccio*—imagined rather than literal views, in which vaguely familiar architectural details are combined with bizarre or imagined elements of a picturesque character.

PIAZZA SAN MARCO
Canaletto (Giovanni Antonio Canal), Italian, Venetian, 1697–1768
Oil on canvas, 27 x 44¼ in.
Purchase, Mrs. Charles Wrightsman Gift, 1988   1988.162

These poetic musings on the Venetian landscape are evocative of many passages of *The Four Seasons*, whose verses frequently call to mind Canaletto's sun-dappled skies and Guardi's stormy, wind-tossed horizons. Nowhere has the beauty and allure of Vivaldi's Venice been more supremely captured than in their works.

Linda Wolk-Simon
Assistant Curator, Robert Lehman Collection
The Metropolitan Museum of Art

2

La Primavera A Giunt' é la Primavera

CONCERTO I

Allegro Pt

Forte **B** Canto dè gl' Vcelli

m, m. m. m. m. m.

t.

Solo

1 t. t. e Festoset

La Salutan gli Augei con lieto canto t. t.

t. t. t. Tutti

Ei fonti allo Spirar de Zef
Scorrono i Fonti

t **C**

Con dolce mormorio Scorrono in tanto *Piano*

D Tuoni, Ve

Forte

SPRING

Spring has come and the cheerful birds
Welcome it with a happy song.

*Giunt' é la Primavera e festosetti
La Salutan gl'Augei con lieto canto,*

And the streams, blown by soft winds,
Flow with a sweet murmur.

Ei fonti allo Spirar de' Zeffiretti
Con dolce mormorio Scorrono intanto

WASHERWOMEN (detail)
François Boucher, French, 1703–1770
Oil on canvas; 95 x 93 in., 1768
Gift of Julia A. Berwind, 1953   53.225.2

Lightning and thunder, chosen to announce the spring,
Come covering the sky with a thick, black mantle.

Vengon' coprendo l'aer di nero amanto
E Lampi, e tuoni ad annuntiarla eletti

But when all is quiet, the birds
Take up their charming song once more.

Indi tacendo questi, gl'Augelletti;
Tornan' di nuovo allor canoro incanto:

Then on the pleasant, flowery meadow,

To the sweet murmuring of plants and leaves,

The goatherd sleeps, his faithful dog beside him.

E quindi Sul fiorito ameno prato
Al caro mormorio di fronde e piante
Dorme'l Caprar col fido can' à lato.

To the festive sound of the pastoral bagpipe,
Nymphs and shepherds dance beneath the beloved
Canopy of spring that so brilliantly now emerges.

Di pastoral Zampogna al Suon festante
Danzan Ninfe e Pastor nel tetto amato
Di primavera all'apparir brillante

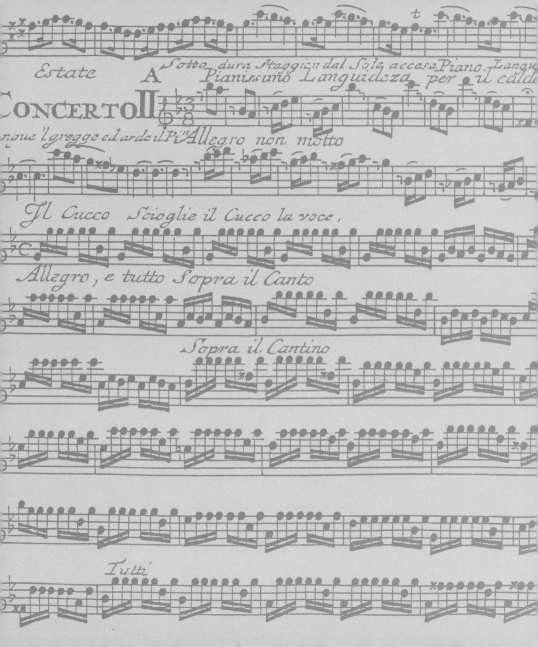

SUMMER

Under the harsh season of the scorching sun,
Man and flock languish and the pine tree burns.

Sotto dura Staggion dal Sole accesa
Langue L'huom, langue 'l gregge, ed arde il Pino;

The cuckoo loosens its voice and, once heard,
The turtledove and goldfinch join in song.

Scioglie il Cucco la Voce, e tosto intesa
Canta la Tortorella e 'l gardelino

The sweet Zephyr blows but once provoked,
The Boreal moves in against its neighbor.

Zeffiro dolce Spira, mà contesa
Muove Borea improviso al Suo vicino;

And the shepherd weeps because he fears
The fierce storm about him and his destiny.

E piange il Pastorel, perche Sospesa
Teme fiera borasca, e'l Suo destino;

Fear of the lightning, the fierce thundering,
And a furious swarm of flies and horseflies,
Disturb the repose of his weary limbs.

Toglie alle membra lasse il Suo riposo
Il timore de' Lampi, e tuoni fieri
E de mosche, e mossoni il Stuol furioso!

Alas, his fears prove only too true.
The sky thunders and flashes, and hail
Lops off ears of corn and lofty grains.

Ah che pur troppo i Suoi timor Son veri
Tuona e fulmina il Ciel e grandinoso
Tronca il capo alle Spiche e a'grani altori

Celebra il vilanel con Violino Principale balli e can
Autumno
A
Ballo e Canto de' Villanelli
CONCERTO III
Allegro
Piano
il bel piacere
Forte
Piano
Solo
Forte
L' Vbriaco
Tutti
B
E del liquor di Bacco
Solo
3

AUTUMN

With dances and songs the peasant celebrates
The great pleasure of a good harvest.

*Celebra il Vilanel con balli e Canti
Del felice raccolto il bel piacere*

Previous page: A PICNIC
Edmé Charles de Lioux de Savignac, French, active ca. 1766–1772
Watercolor and gouache on paper; Diam. 3 in.
Bequest of Mary Clark Thompson, 1923   24.80.527

A DANCE IN THE COUNTRY (detail)
Giovanni Domenico Tiepolo, Italian, Venetian, 1727–1804
Oil on canvas; 29¾ x 47¼ in.
Gift of Mr. and Mrs. Charles Wrightsman, 1980   1980.67

And many, ablaze from Bacchus' liquor,
Finish their merriment in sleep.

E del liquor di Bacco accesi tanti
Finiscono col Sonno il lor godere

THE PICNIC AFTER THE HUNT (detail)
Carle (Charles André) Vanloo, French, 1705–1765
Oil on canvas; 23¼ x 19½ in.
Wrightsman Fund, 1995   1995.317

Now the mild and pleasant air
Makes everyone give up dancing and singing.

Fà ch'ogn' uno tralasci e balli e canti
L'aria che temperata dà piacere,

CONCERT CHAMPÊTRE (detail)
Jean Baptiste Joseph Pater, French, 1695–1736
Oil on canvas; 20½ x 26¾ in.
Purchase, Joseph Pulitzer Bequest, 1937   37.27

It is the season that invites one and all
To the great joys of a sweet deep sleep.

E la Staggion ch' invita tanti e tanti
D'un dolcissimo Sonno al bel godere.

At daybreak the hunters are off to hunt,
With horns, rifles, and dogs they head outside.
The wild beast flees and they follow in its tracks;

I cacciator alla nov' alba à caccia
Con corni, Schioppi, e canni escono fuore
Fugge la belua, e Seguono la traccia;

Already stunned and weary from the din
Of rifles and dogs, the wounded beast threatens,
Weakly trying to flee, but dies, overwhelmed.

Già Sbigottita, e lassa al gran rumore
De' Schioppi e canni, ferita minaccia
Languida di fuggir, mà oppressa muore

Dog Guarding Dead Game (detail)
Jean Baptiste Oudry, Flemish, 1686–1755
Oil on canvas; $25\frac{1}{2}$ x $31\frac{3}{4}$ in., 1753
Purchase, 1871 71.89

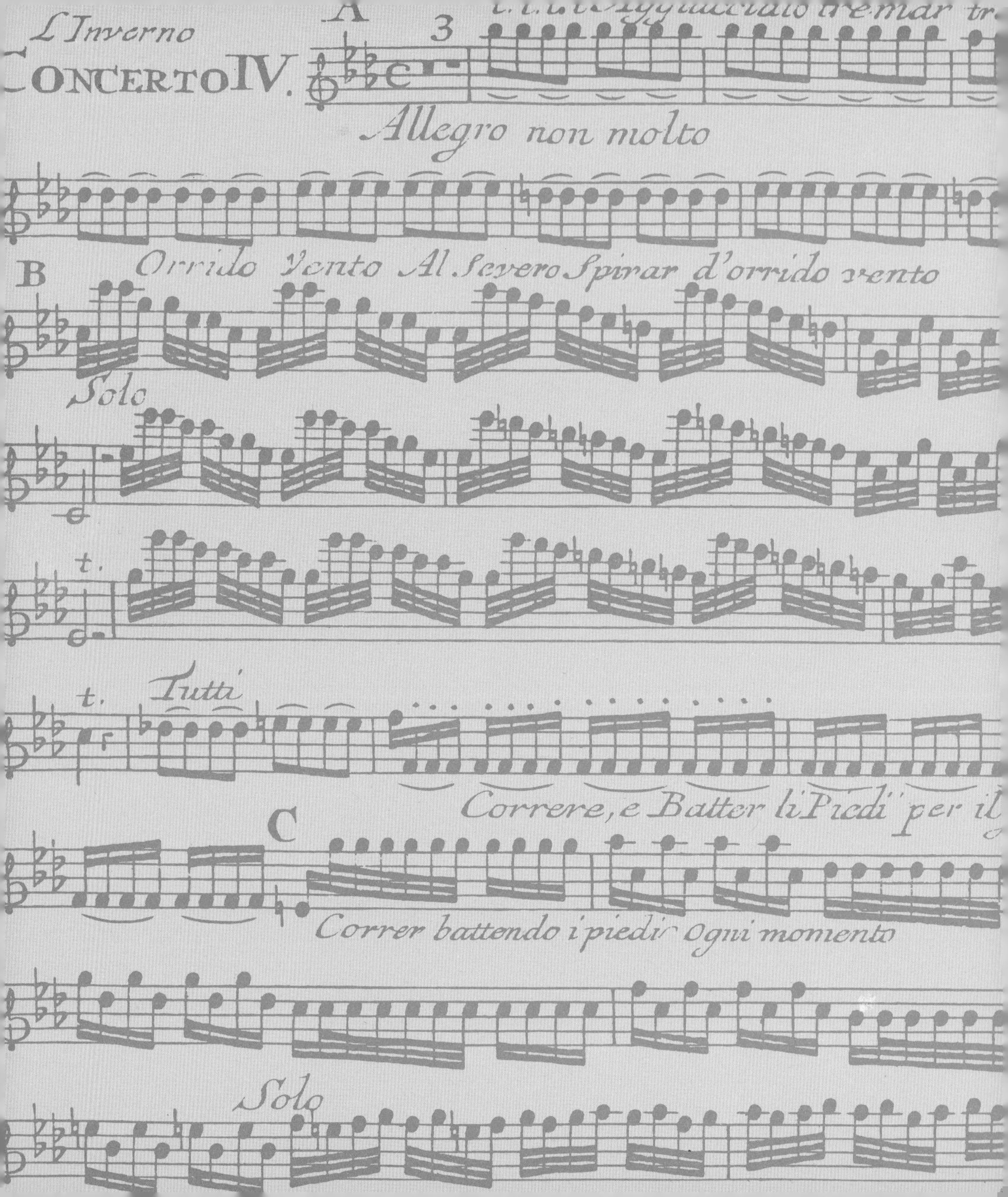

L'Inverno
CONCERTO IV.
A
3
agghiacciato tremar
Allegro non molto
B
Orrido Vento Al Severo Spirar d'orrido vento
Solo
t.
t.
Tutti
Correre, e Batter li Piedi per il
C
Correr battendo i piedi Ogni momento
Solo

WINTER

To tremble, frozen from the icy snow
Amid the biting breath of the horrid wind,

Aggiacciato tremar trà nevi algenti
Al Severo Spirar d' orrido Vento,

To run, stamping our feet at every turn
And chattering our teeth in the hard frost;

Correr battendo i piedi ogni momento;
E pel Soverchio gel batter i denti;

To pass quiet, serene days before the fire,
While outside the rain pours ceaselessly down,

Passar al foco i di quieti e contenti
Mentre la pioggio fuor bagna ben cento

To walk over the ice with a slow step,
Moving with care for fear of falling through.

Caminar Sopra 'l giaccio, e à passo lento
Per timor di cader gersene intenti;

To turn sharply, slip, fall to the ground
Then go out again on the ice and dash about
Until the ice breaks and splits open,

Gir forte Sdruzziolar, cader à terra
Di nuovo ir Sopra'l giaccio e correr forte
Sin ch' il giaccio Si rompe, e Si disserra;

To hear the Sirocco, Boreas, and all the winds
Break through iron-clad doors and clash in war.
This is the winter, but what a joy it brings.

Sentir uscir dalle ferrate porte
Sirocco Barea, e tutti i Venti in guerra
Quest' e'l verno, mà tal, che gioja apporte

Antonio Vivaldi (1678–1741)
The Four Seasons

Spring (*La primavera*), op. 8, no. 1
Concerto in E major, RV 269

1. **Allegro:** *Giunt'è la primavera* (Spring has come)—*Canto degl'uccelli* (Song of the birds)—*Scorrono i fonti* (Streams flow)—*Tuoni* (Thunder)—*Canto d'uccelli* (Song of the birds)   [3:12]

2. **Largo e pianissimo:** *Il capraio che dorme* (The goatherd sleeps)—*Mormorio di fronde e piante* (Murmuring leaves and plants)—*Il cane che grida* (The barking dog)   [2:44]

3. **Allegro:** *Danza pastorale* (Pastoral dance)   [3:50]

Summer (*L'estate*), op. 8, no. 2
Concerto in G minor, RV 315

4. **Allegro ma non molto:** *Languidezza per il caldo* (Languished by the heat)—*Il cucco* (The cuckoo)—*La tortorella* (The turtledove)—*Il cardellino* (The goldfinch)—*Zeffiretti dolci* (Sweet breezes)—*Venti diversi* (Various winds)–*Vento borea* (North wind)—*Il pianto del villanello* (The peasant boy's tears)   [4:36]

5. **Adagio—Presto:** *Mosche e mossoni* (Flies and horseflies)   [2:20]

6. **Presto:** *Tempo impetuoso d'estate* (Violent summer weather)   [2:36]

Autumn (*L'autunno*), op. 8, no. 3
Concerto in F major, RV 293

7. **Allegro:** *Ballo e canto de' villanelli* (Peasants' dance and song)—*L'ubriaco* (The drinker)—*L'ubriaco che dorme* (The drinker sleeps)   [5:05]

8. **Adagio molto:** *Ubriachi dormenti* (Drinkers sleep)   [2:43]

9. **Allegro:** *La caccia* (The hunt)—*La fiera che fugge* (The fleeing beast)—*Schioppi e cani* (Guns and dogs)—*La fiera, fuggendo, muoro* (The fleeing beast is slain)   [3:06]

Winter (*L'inverno*), op. 8, no. 4
Concerto in F minor, RV 297

10. **Allegro ma non molto:** *Agghiacciato tremar tra nevi algenti* (Trembling in the icy snow)—*Orrido vento* (Horrid wind)—*Batter de' piedi per il freddo* (Stamping feet in the cold)—*Venti* (Winds)–*Batter li denti* (Chattering teeth)   [3:12]

11. **Largo:** *La pioggia* (Rain)   [1:55]

12. **Allegro:** *Camminar sopra il ghiaccio* (Walking on ice)—*Camminar piano e con timore* (Moving with care)—*Cader a terra* (Falling down)—*Correr forte* (Dashing about)—*Il vento sirocco* (The hot desert wind)—*Il vento borea e tutti li venti* (The cold north wind and all the winds)   [2:43]

Paul Peabody, violin

Concerto in C major for Mandolin, Strings, and Continuo, RV 425

13. **Allegro**   [2:45]
14. **Largo**   [3:42]
15. **Allegro**   [2:09]

Peter Press, mandolin

PHILHARMONIA VIRTUOSI
RICHARD KAPP, CONDUCTOR

Recording originally released by
ESS.A.Y Recordings

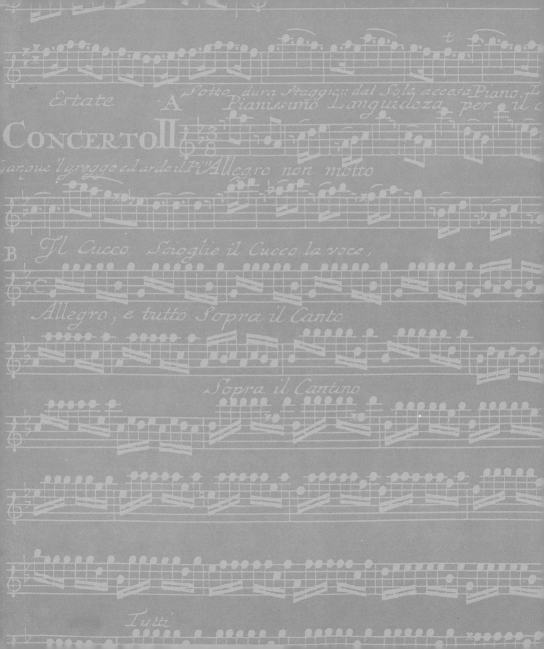